Cornwall's Early Lifeboats

1803-1939

Cyril Noall

Tor Mark Press   Penryn

The Arab *of Padstow, rounding Stepper Point, near where she was wrecked on 11 April 1900*

This edition first published 1989 by Tor Mark Press, Islington Wharf, Penryn, Cornwall, TR10 8AT

Based on *The Story of Cornwall's Lifeboats*

© 1989 Tor Mark Press

ISBN 0-85025-317-9

The photographs in this book are reproduced by kind permission of the Royal Institution of Cornwall. The publishers would like to thank the Royal National Lifeboat Institution for their assistance in compiling this book, and Roger Penhallurick of the Royal Institution of Cornwall for his assistance in picture research

Printed in Great Britain by Swannack Brown Ltd, Hull

Cornwall's Lifeboats up to 1850

In olden days, Cornwall had a fearsome reputation with sailors of all nations. The county's treacherous, storm-lashed coastline was no less dreaded than its rapacious inhabitants, for any vessel coming to grief upon these hazardous shores was almost certain to be stripped and destroyed by the local wreckers. By the beginning of the nineteenth century, however, a new humanitarian spirit was beginning to manifest itself among more enlightened Cornishmen, the first fruits of which were demonstrated in a decision by a number of residents in the neighbourhood of Mount's Bay, to establish a lifeboat at Penzance in 1803. This, the first Cornish **Penzance** lifeboat, was one of thirty built by Henry Greathead, a ship's carpenter, of Shields, and modelled on the famous *Original* of 1789, a 30 ft ten-oared double ended boat with a curved keel, but lacking the self-righting principle.

The Penzance boat was built with a grant of £50 from the Committee at Lloyd's, together with another £100 locally subscribed. It lasted just under nine years, during which time it rendered no service; and in 1812 the boat was taken in distress for rent, and sold for twenty guineas. However, when the Royal National Institution for the Preservation of Life from Shipwreck – the present-day RNLI – was established in 1824, a branch was formed at Penzance, and a new lifeboat provided.

The formation of the National Shipwreck Institution also seems to have stimulated the provision of a lifeboat at Padstow, on the **Padstow** north coast of Cornwall, at about this time. The actual origins of this station are a little obscure, for whilst the Institution's Annual Report for 1824-5 stated that a lifeboat was *planned* for Padstow district, it seems fairly certain that the first boat was not built till 1827 after the merchants and townspeople had made a collection for the purpose. This 1827 lifeboat was only 23 ft long and rowed four oars. She is believed to have been named *Mariner's Friend,* and was probably at first kept on the Quay. Two years later she was installed in a house at Hawker's Cove under the aegis of the Padstow Harbour Association for the Preservation of Life and Property from Shipwreck. This body, unique in Cornwall, was founded in November 1829, and aimed to reduce the hazards of entering this difficult and dangerous harbour. Its chief memorial today is the 40-ft daymark on Stepper Point; but the Association also achieved notable success in its endeavours to rescue ships and their crews. Between November 1830 and February 1831, they 'preserved six vessels from total wreck'; and at their second Annual

General Meeting reported the placing at Stepper Point of 'a substantial six-oar'd boat, well calculated for a heavy sea' – probably a heavy gig – to assist in performing this noble work. This boat participated in a heroic rescue attempt on 29 November 1833, when the brig *Albion,* from Youghal to London, ran on the dreaded 'Dunbar' (Doom Bar) Sands in a most violent gale, her crew of four being saved by the *Mariner's Friend.*

The Association's boat made another outstanding rescue on the morning of 30 November 1836, during a severe north-westerly gale, when the smack *Britannia* and the Welsh schooner *Jane* ran for harbour on the ebb tide. Having reached the apparent shelter of Stepper Point, baffling cross winds caused them to collide and, locked together, they drifted on to the Doom Bar. The smack's master leapt on board the schooner, but at the same instant she struck bottom, and the two vessels parted, the smack driving farther ashore with three men still on board. After rockets had unsuccessfully been fired from shore, the schooner broke up, and the six or seven men on board were thrown into the sea and quickly drowned. The Association's boat then went out to the smack and rescued the three on board, a feat of great heroism.

Bude The next Cornish lifeboat station to be established was that at Bude, in 1837. Bude lies in the centre of a stretch of coastline notorious for the frequency of its shipwrecks, for, as that grim old couplet so well known to the seamen in sailing ship days has it,

> From Padstow Point to Lundy Light,
> Is a watery grave by day or night.

The station's inception was the direct outcome of two wrecks which occurred on the same day – 29 October 1836 – one of them being the *Providence,* a packet plying between Wexford and Bristol, and the other an unknown schooner lost two miles out at sea, in each case without the saving of a single survivor. *Felix Farley's Bristol Journal* of 26 November that year, wrote:

> We have authority to state that, when the circumstance was reported to the King and that no means were provided even for endeavouring to save the lives of his subjects in such extreme peril, on the coast, too, so remarkable for shipwrecks that even in the life time of one man nearly forty are known to have occurred, his Majesty most promptly and munificently commanded that a sum of money should be give from the Duchy of Cornwall for the purpose of establishing a life-boat at Bude.

The craft was built by the well-known boat-builder, Wake, of Sunderland, and was of the 'North Country' type of surf boat, for rowing only, based on the original Greathead design. Unfortunately, she did not find favour with the local boatmen, and her career consequently was not a happy one. Only one record of a service launch is known, when in October 1843 two brigs were wrecked at Bude during a strong WNW gale. One, the *Favourite,* bound from Cardiff to Rotterdam, with iron, drove ashore at the back of the breakwater, her crew being rescued from the shore. The other brig, the *Alonzo,* came on shore on the sands nearly opposite the harbour without a soul on board. She was bound for Hamburg with iron, and had left Cardiff at the same time as the *Favourite.* The crew of nine had previously abandoned her off Morwenstow in their boat, which was immediately swamped in the terrible seas, all being drowned. The *Alonzo* became deeply embedded in the sands, and on the following day, when the sea had subsided, she was visited by a crew in the lifeboat. It can hardly be without significance that this craft was not employed to rescue the men on the *Favourite,* and did not visit the *Alonzo* till all danger was past.

Whatever little confidence the Bude lifeboatmen may have had in her must have been completely destroyed by a calamity which occurred during a practice launch on 10 October 1844. When rowing her at the northern side of the harbour, a sudden heavy surge broke the steersman's oar and four others on the port side, bringing the boat broadside on to the sea; a second big wave capsized her, throwing some of the crew into the water. Several men were trapped beneath the boat where they remained until she came into shallow water, where a rescue party turned her over and rescued them. Another saved himself by clinging to the bottom of the upturned boat, whilst two more were rescued by a shore boat. Two lifeboatmen, however, were drowned.

Another lifeboat station was opened in 1837 at the opposite end **St Mary's** of the county – at St Mary's, Scilly. Provided by the National Shipwreck Institution, this boat was in charge of the Inspecting Commander of the Coast Guard, Capt Charles Steel, RN, but it lasted only three years, being replaced in 1840 by one transferred from the Plymouth station. She was of the type designed by Pellew Plenty, of Newbury, the first 'standard' boat adopted by the Institution, and had been built in 1828. She was 26 ft long, pulled ten oars, and like her predecessor was kept in a stone house fronting the Town Beach at Thorofare.

Steel himself led the crew of this second boat on their only recorded service. Just before seven on the morning of 4 January 1841, the steam packet *Thames,* from Dublin to London, was seen to the west, apparently disabled, and lying at the mercy of a westerly gale, which was relentlessly driving her into a position of extreme danger. Seas had found their way below, putting out the boiler fires. In this helpless state, she eventually struck Jacky's Rock – a part of the reef which stands like a wall at the south-west of the islands, the Western Rocks. The crew fired blue lights to summon help, and rescue preparations were at once made at St Agnes and St Mary's. The St Agnes gig *Thomas* was first launched, followed by the *Bee* **St Agnes** and *Briton,* and later, the pilot cutter *Active.*

5

At St Mary's, Capt Steel called for volunteers. After slight delay, the lifeboat put off, and, like the gigs, struggled against mountainous seas and through squalls of hail and sleet. The *Thomas* reached the scene first, and managed to save three women on board. Then a sudden squall whipped up the waves, and with the boat tossing and plunging uncontrollably it became impossible to maintain contact. The women were transferred to another boat and taken back to St Agnes. The remaining boats hovered near the wreck, waiting for any chance of a lull during which they could close in for a rescue, but were frustrated. Some twenty or so army recruits on the *Thames* eventually launched the two ship's boats, but every soul perished. The sailors lashed together rafts, and as the mainmast of the *Thames* broke adrift, tearing up the decks and completing the destructive work of the waves in a few minutes, they floated off, only to be upset and dashed ashore on Rosevear. Only one man survived the night, by sheltering inside a cask stuffed with grass. The lifeboat herself landed a couple of men, whilst from the rocks and the sea eight bodies were collected and brought to St Mary's for burial. Altogether, about 57 lives were lost in this disaster. The Institution awarded its gold medal to Steel, its silver medal to each of the original four volunteers in the lifeboat, and cash rewards to the others in the lifeboat and the crews of the gigs.

St Ives   Turning again to the Cornish mainland, the Shipwreck Society in 1838 awarded five silver medals to volunteers who participated in the heroic rescue of the crew of the schooner *Rival,* which grounded at the back of Smeaton's Pier, St Ives, during a heavy gale on the afternoon of December 24th. Local pilots first attempted to save the crew by putting off in three six-oared gigs, but failed; rocket-firing apparatus also proved ineffectual, owing to the distance to be covered. Two fishing boats then tried to board her, but were swept to leeward on to Porthminster Beach. The gig *Rasper* then succeeded, after various attempts and at great risk, in getting within a few yards of the vessel, but was then nearly filled by a tremendous sea and drove ashore, capsizing near Pednolver Rocks, the crew narrowly escaping with their lives. A pilchard tow-boat was then launched, and got near enough to the *Rival* to lay hold of a rope. Before they could make it fast, however, a heavy sea forced their boat to leeward. When again attempting to reach the vessel another tremendous sea washed two men overboard who were miraculously saved by their comrades. The boat, minus several oars, and nearly full of water, finally drove ashore and upset on the beach. It was re-launched with a fresh-crew, and again got near the vessel, but was driven back by the violence of the surf. The crew resumed their oars, and at length succeeded in getting off the *Rival's* crew of five, and landing them on Porthminster Beach as darkness was falling. They later managed to get the schooner off and brought her to the pier.

In the same year, 1838, the Royal Cornwall Polytechnic Society conducted a competition for the best designed model lifeboat sent for their inspection. The first two awards were won by entries from St Ives, the premium offered by Mr Charles Fox going to Mr Francis Jennings Adams (1769-1845), a well-known local shipbuilder, and the second prize of two guineas to Mr John Phillips, schoolmaster. A full size lifeboat, made to Adams' design, was later built by Adams himself and stationed at St Ives. Fitted with two bows, she was steered by an oar at either end, there being six rowers in addition who were able to change direction by turning round on the same thwarts. The boat was clinker-built, and fitted up like a gig, with bottom boards and stretchers, whilst cork lining and air tanks ensured its buoyancy. Named the *Hope,* her first launch took place on 11 January 1840.

Her first – and only known – service launch which took place in April 1840, proved to be a gallant failure. During a northerly gale, the smack *Mary Ann,* of Poole, laden with coal from Swansea, drove on shore near Pednolver Point, the mast soon after going by the board. In two attempts to reach the vessel the lifeboat was thrown back upon the beach by the violence of the sea and filled with water. Two men then swam off to the smack, and at the imminent risk of their own lives, succeeded in saving the crew.

From 1850 to 1900

In 1850 there were only five lifeboat stations active along the whole seaboard of Cornwall; and of these one or two had already lapsed after the fading of the initial burst of enthusiasm. Matters were soon, however, to take a turn for the better. Following the publication of the Northumberland Report of 1851, which revealed not only the achievements but also the serious deficiencies of the lifeboat service at that time, a considerable number of new stations were inaugurated, no less than fourteen being commissioned in Cornwall before 1870.

The first of this new group was opened at Sennen Cove, near **Sennen** Land's End, in 1853. The decision to place a lifeboat here was doubtless stimulated by the heroic efforts of local fishermen, coastguards and revenue officers in attempting to save the lives of the crew and captain's wife of the snow *New Commercial,* wrecked on the fearful Brisons rocks in January 1851. In connection with this, Capt George Davies, RN, Inspecting Commander of the Coastguard at Penzance, and Mr Forward, of the revenue cruiser *Sylvia* were each awarded the RNLI's highly coveted gold medal; whilst eleven others received silver medals.

The first Sennen lifeboat measured 25 ft 8 ins and rowed six oars. She arrived at Sennen in June, 1853, being conveyed to Penzance by

One of three Lizard lifeboats named Anna Maria. *From the evidence of the clothes, this photograph appears to be from the 1860s*

steamer and from there towed to her destination by the local revenue cruiser. This boat performed only one service, of minor importance; but her successor, the *Cousins William and Mary Ann of Bideford,* participated in one of the most dramatic rescues effected at this station when on 23 October 1868 the Government lighter *Devon* shared the fate of the *New Commercial* and was totally wrecked on the Brisons. Only one of the eighteen on board managed to save himself by taking refuge in a cleft in the rocks. Early next morning the St Just coastguard observed him in this perilous position, and the lifeboat put out to rescue him. Despite appalling weather conditions, he was eventually saved by lifebuoy after a line had been fired by rocket from the lifeboat.

Lizard   Second only to Land's End as one of the most exposed promontories on our coasts, the Lizard has exacted a terrible toll of shipping; but it was not until 1859 that a lifeboat station was opened there, at Polpeor Cove. The stimulating cause, in this case, appears to have been the wreck of the iron steamer *Czar,* of Hull, on the submerged Vrogue rock on 22 January 1859. The Lizard coastguards put off at great risk and picked up five or six floating in the sea; and one boat's crew from the *Czar* landed safely at one of the coves; but another boat, with nine or ten survivors, was swamped and all in her drowned.

The first Lizard lifeboat, named *Anna Maria,* arrived on station in November 1859 having been sent to Falmouth on board a steam packet. Thence she was taken on her carriage by road to the Lizard. She was a 30 ft self-righter, rowing six oars. On 2 January 1866, when on a quarterly exercise, she was unfortunately wrecked with the loss of three gallant men, being replaced by another boat identical in name and size with the first. A third *Anna Maria,* placed on station in 1873, was responsible for saving 27 lives from the ss *Mosel,* 3,200 tons, bound from Bremen via Southampton, for New York, wrecked below the signal station in dense fog in August 1882. She carried about 600 passengers, a crew of 100, and a cargo which included valuable bullion. One of the officers leapt ashore and climbed the cliff to summon help. Besides the lifeboat, the ship's own nine boats were soon launched, and the Falmouth tug, *Rosette,* came alongside. The tug took the coin, mails, and some saloon passengers to Falmouth.

In 1885 the *Anna Maria* was transferred to a new station at Church Cove, where the launching arrangements were very difficult, and only one service launch was performed there. At Polpeor, a new lifeboat arrived in 1885, named *Edmund and Fanny.* On 28 September 1886 she performed a valuable rescue operation in conjunction with the Cadgwith lifeboat when the ss *Suffolk,* 2,924 tons, was wrecked in dense fog. The crew and passengers got away in the ship's boats, from which they were transferred to the lifeboats, and all were landed at Polpeor.

In 1892 a new boathouse was completed nearer the beach; the boat could be launched down a path of greased skids, greatly speeding the operation. This alteration followed two cases of wrecks in which the crews got ashore in their own boats, showing the need for more rapid means of getting the lifeboat afloat.

Polkerris

In the same year that the Lizard station was opened, another lifeboat was placed further to the eastward along the south Cornish coast, at Polkerris, in St Austell Bay. At that period, sailing ships visited several small harbours in the vicinity – among them Charlestown, Par and Fowey – in order to load china clay; and as the coastline was a tricky one for navigation, wrecks were not infrequent. The wreck of the *Endeavour,* in 1856 led to a demand being made for a lifeboat to be placed in the area; and after generous donations had been made by several of the local gentry a station was inaugurated at the little fishing village of Polkerris in 1859. The first lifeboat, named *Catherine Rashleigh,* was forwarded by rail to Lostwithiel, then rowed down the river Fowey and round Gribbin Head to her station, being afterwards rowed round the bay and exhibited to enthusiastic crowds at Charlestown and Par.

On 25 November 1865, this lifeboat performed a classic service when two vessels, the barque *Drydens,* and the brig *Wearmouth* were both wrecked on Par Sands when attempting to make Par harbour in a strong southerly gale. The *Catherine Rashleigh*, with Chief Boatman Joshua Heath of the coastguard in charge, had been launched as soon as the vessels were seen being driven mercilessly into the bay. The oarsmen were struggling mightily and the gale was increasing. When about half way to their goal they were caught by a particularly heavy sea which snatched six oars from their hands. Coxswain Heath allowed the boat to drift some way to leeward and then hoisted his sails, intending to make for Par. Unfortunately, seeing the lifeboat sailing away, the crew of the brig despaired of being rescued. They launched their boat and two men got into it, but one afterwards took fright and returned to the brig, whilst the other, who got adrift, was rescued by the lifeboat which altered course for this purpose. They were amazed to find the ship's cat clinging to him, a dishevelled, frightened bundle of fur. They landed the man and cat at Par and took on board fresh oars. The barque now being in urgent need of help, they made for her and took off the whole crew of thirteen. Having landed these, and replaced two exhausted lifeboatmen, they went out again to the brig and succeeded in rescuing the eight persons still on board, to the ringing cheers of spectators on the pierhead. The silver medal of the RNLI was awarded to Coxswain Heath for this fine service.

Newquay   During the middle of the last century, Newquay, the popular holiday resort on the north coast, was one of the centres of the Cornish pilchard seining industry. The adjacent coastline was the scene of repeated wrecks and during the 1850s local coastguards performed no less than three rescues which won the award of the Institution's silver medal. With the need for a lifeboat at Newquay thus clearly established, a station was opened there in 1861, the first boat being named *Joshua*. After performing one service, she was condemned, having fallen vicitim to dry rot, her successor in 1865 being given the same name. This second *Joshua* was involved in some lively proceedings when the Austrian barque *Suez* anchored in distress off Newquay on 20 December 1869. All the vessel's crew of ten were taken into the lifeboat and brought safely ashore. Meanwhile, the *Suez* continued to ride at anchor in Watergate Bay, and on the following day attempts were made to save her. A salvage tug was ordered from Cardiff for the purpose; but local boatmen refused to obey the orders of the Receiver of Wreck, that they should not put off to her themselves, until warned that they could be shot if they attempted to move her. Coastguards and officials then launched the lifeboat amid a hostile crowd who threatened anyone prepared to accompany them, though £5 was offered to each volunteer. As a result, the lifeboat was left aground by the ebbing tide in the harbour. Eventually the tug brought two boats and crews from Padstow, who carried out the salvage operation. A contemporary account states that 'there was a chorus of yells,

Until 1895 Newquay's lifeboats were drawn through the streets of the town to be launched

execrations, and the usual accompaniment of an attempt at mob rule, during which time the ship was kept in a very dangerous position'.

Until 1895 the Newquay lifeboat was kept in a boathouse in Fore Street, but during that year a new house was built for it near the end of the bold headland which protects the harbour from westerly gales. Here she was able to slide into deep water within easy reach of the open sea and in command of the whole Bay.

In 1863 the little seaport and fishing harbour of Porthleven, in **Porthleven** Mount's Bay, was provided with a lifeboat. Named after her donor, *Agar-Robartes,* she performed her first service on 5 December 1866, when the Finnish barque *Salmi* was seen in a dangerous position and apparently making for the land. The lifeboat launched into a heavy sea and, getting alongside, placed four of her own crew on board, who helped to get the barque into Falmouth harbour.

The station at Looe dates from 1866. The first lifeboat placed **Looe** there was named *Oxfordshire,* her cost met from a collection made among residents of the county of Oxford. During the afternoon of

11

*The inaugural ceremony at Penzance for the Mullion lifeboat
D J Draper, on 10 September 1867*

14 December 1868, the schooner *Mail* appeared off the port in
distress during a strong SW gale. The lifeboat was successfully
launched through heavy surf and brought the vessel with her crew
of six safely into the harbour. This valuable though unspectacular
service was typical of the work performed by lifeboats of this
station over the years.

Hayle   The Hayle station was opened in the same year as Looe; and
curiously, there was a connection again with Oxford – the city and
University, in this case, rather than the county. The first boat was
provided by a fund collected by the Rev G S Ward, of Magdalen Hall.
On 24 April 1866, after being drawn on her carriage through the
principal streets of Oxford, she was taken to the towing path of the
river and manned by the University Eight, victors in that year's boat
race. During the subsequent ceremony she received the
appropriate name *Isis*. At Hayle she performed several notable
services. During the great March gale of 1869 the brig *Lizzie* struck
on the Stones near Godrevy and grounded at midnight on the
eastern spit of Hayle Bar. A heavy sea swept away the two men at the
wheel, one of whom was drowned. In response to signals, the St
Ives lifeboat *Moses* was drawn overland to the western side of the
Bar, launched into the river and pulled seaward. The *Isis* reached
the wreck first, however, pulling through a heavy sea, but found it

impossible to get alongside. The *Lizzie's* crew managed to float a keg with a line attached to the Hayle boat, which was then drawn to the wreck, and the crew rescued under exceedingly difficult and dangerous circumstances.

The station at Mullion was another with which the name of T J **Mullion** Agar Robartes was closely associated. Largely through his efforts, a lifeboat was placed there in 1867, named *D J Draper.* The inaugural ceremony, however, did not take place at Mullion, but at Penzance, when she was drawn through the streets in procession with lifeboats from Penzance, St Ives and Hayle. Together with other boats from Porthleven and Sennen, these participated in a lifeboat race, watched by a crowd estimated at ten thousand. Only one successful service was performed by the Mullion station, when on 21 October 1867 the *D J Draper* saved three lives from the Scottish barque *Achilles.*

Falmouth received its first lifeboat in the same year as Mullion. **Falmouth** Christened *City of Gloucester,* she was a gift of the people of that place. Her impressive inauguration ceremony at Falmouth took place on 28 August. The lifeboat, drawn by twelve horses, left the docks and paraded the town with a full crew as far as Penryn, accompanied by a procession which included several bands. This station, however, had a remarkably barren record during the nineteenth century; only one life-saving service was performed during the first 34 years of its existence, in February 1895, when the *Bob Newborn* lifeboat rescued four from the schooner *Aneurin.* It has subsequently, however, achieved a magnificent record of service.

The third Cornish station to be opened in 1869 was at Cadgwith, **Cadgwith** on the eastern side of the Lizard peninsula. The original lifeboat here was given the curious name of *Western Commercial Traveller,* having been purchased by a subscription among commercial travellers in the West of England. On 9 February 1869, this boat launched to the assistance of a large disabled ship about seven miles off. They quickly reached her under canvas, the WSW gale then blowing being in their favour. Despite the wreckage alongside, they eventually got under her quarter and took off the eight men who were left on board. As the ship was rolling heavily in the trough of the seas, this took some time, and while two men caught the survivors as they jumped down, practically all hands were required to fend the lifeboat away from the towering iron hull. Having at last got the men on board, they pulled clear, signalled to the Lizard lifeboat that the job was completed, and then both had to run for Falmouth. The ship was the Black Ball liner *Calcutta,* bound from London to the Persian Gulf with telegraph cable which they were to lay at sea. The *Calcutta* had previously been in collision with the brig *Emma* which foundered, only four of her crew managing to get on board the ship. The *Calcutta* began to make water, and several boats got away with various members of the crew, leaving only the eight who were eventually rescued by lifeboat. One of the ship's boats was driven ashore in pieces on Mullion Island, all 21 on board being drowned. Two others reached land, whilst the men in the fourth were rescued at sea by the French schooner *Lucy.* Of the 64 in the *Calcutta's* complement, 33 were drowned.

Porthoustock   Cruellest of all the submerged reefs with which Cornwall guards its ironbound coastline is the Manacles, lying between a quarter of a mile and a mile offshore between Porthoustock and Lowland Points, on the western approach to Falmouth harbour. How many scores of vessels, how many hundreds of lives, have been lost upon these rocks is a matter of conjecture; but the figures must far exceed those for any comparable stretch of water off the British mainland. One need but give a brief roll-call of the most famous wrecks here – *Primrose, Dispatch, John, Andola, Mohegan, Paris* – to underline this point. In an attempt to mitigate such disasters, the RNLI in 1869 placed a lifeboat in the then quaint and unspoilt fishing village of Porthoustock. Named *Mary Ann Story,* the boat with a full crew on board was drawn through Helston by a team of nine horses *en route* to her station, the inaugural ceremony taking place on 29 September. In November 1877, this boat saved 23 from the ship *Ceres,* of Greenock, in a very gallant service. Her successor, the *Charlotte,* was associated with three of the most notable disasters in this area – the *Andola,* in January 1895; the *Mohegan,* in October 1898; and the *Paris,* in May 1899.

Port Isaac   The station at Port Isaac was established in 1869 mainly to afford better protection for the fishing boats of this and adjacent coves which often had to run for harbour at great risk in bad weather. The first three lifeboats here were each called *Richard and Sarah.* The earliest of these boats saved 25 lives on 14 October 1886, when the ss *Indus,* bound from Cardiff to Tenerife with coal, foundered off Trevose. The lifeboat found two of her boats, containing the crew of 29 and a stowaway, drifting along the coast. She took on board all except five of these who were brought back by a fishing vessel. Several other notable services were performed by boats from this station, among which may be mentioned the Penzance schooner *Golden Light* in 1890 (5 saved) and the barque *Antoinette,* of New Brunswick in 1895 (10 saved).

Mevagissey   The little fishing port of Mevagissey was also supplied with a lifeboat in 1869. The boat was actually kept around the headland at Port Melon; the first to be stationed there bore the name *South Warwickshire.* On the last day of 1869 she performed a meritorious service when the French brigantine *Girondin,* bound from Bordeaux to Belfast with maize, appeared in distress off Chapel Point, driving before the wind right into the bay. The lifeboat was launched through the surf but the breakers hurled her back on to

Mevagissey's South Warwickshire, *at Port Mellon in 1869, when her service began*

the beach. In attempting to get the boat back on the carriage several helpers nearly lost their lives, being struck down by the seas. Eventually the boat was successfully got afloat, and away towards the casualty, every sea washing clean over her. The *South Warwickshire,* in fact, had to be driven half a mile through breaking seas with the drogue streaming aft to reach the vessel. The *Girondin* was aground a long way inside the bar with furious seas breaking over her, and the crew had taken refuge in the rigging. The lifeboat was thrice completely buried by the seas but the crew, numbering six, were successfully taken off by the lifeboatmen, and landed at Par.

In 1870, a lifeboat was sent to Portloe, on the SW side of Veryan Bay, to provide intermediate cover between Falmouth and Mevagissey. The site chosen was a poor one, owing to the bad access to Portloe, and the station consequently proved a complete failure, the lifeboat *Gorfenkle* being withdrawn in 1887 without having performed a service.

Portloe

Mary Ann Story *at Porthoustock* ▶

15

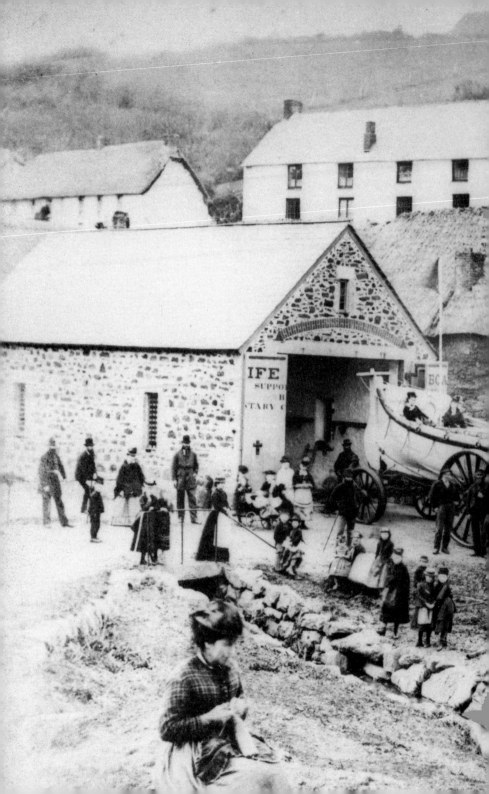

St Agnes   The last Cornish lifeboat station opened during the last century was at St Agnes, on the Isles of Scilly in 1890. This was established at Priglis Bay, mainly with the object of attending wrecks on the Western Rocks, which have claimed more victims than any other part of the islands. The first boat here was the ten-oared 34 ft *James and Caroline*. Her first service took place during the tremendous blizzard which struck the West Country from 9-12 March 1891. At 4.30 pm on the 10th the smack *Porth,* of Padstow, was observed disabled by the loss of sails and at the mercy of the NE gale which raged thick with snow. She struck before the lifeboat could reach her, and one man jumped overboard, swam to a rock, but was unfortunately washed off and drowned. The smack drifted away again and stranded on Annet, her skipper and remaining hand landing in their own boat. When the lifeboat took them on board they were completely exhausted from their battering in the blizzard and subsequent efforts to get to the islet in their boat.

Padstow   So much for the new stations established during this half-century. Meanwhile, valuable work continued to be done at the older stations. At Padstow, in particular, a noble record of life-saving was achieved, marred, unfortunately, by two terrible lifeboat disasters. The first occurred on 6 February 1867, when the schooner *Georgiana* and a crew of five was wrecked on the Doom Bar. The lifeboat was launched under oars, but in attempting to approach the wreck four of these were broken. With the tide rushing out through the narrows making it impossible to return, Coxswain Hills headed across the harbour, hoping to beach his boat at Polzeath. However, seas repeatedly filled the boat, more oars were broken, and the canvas of the drogue split, causing her to capsize. Eight of the crew were saved, some by persons bravely dashing into the surf, but five were drowned. The *Georgiana* meanwhile drifted to the shore, her crew in the rigging. One fell into the sea and was drowned, but a baulk of timber was later floated to shore with a line, enabling a hawser to be passed, and by this means the remainder of the crew were saved.

In 1899 Padstow station was supplied with a powerful 56 ft long steam lifeboat, screw propelled. She was kept moored, her function being to assist at wrecks along the coast which were beyond the ability of the rowing and sailing boat kept at Hawker's Cove. On 11 April 1900, the trawling ketch *Peace and Plenty* was driven on the rocks off Greenaway on a strong WNW wind. Several of the crew were rescued by rocket apparatus: one swam ashore; and three others were drowned. Meanwhile, the *Arab* rowing lifeboat had put off to warn the ketch of her danger, but was herself wrecked in the attempt, all thirteen of her crew fortunately getting safely ashore. Seeing a flare which had been put up by the *Arab,* the steam lifeboat went out beyond Stepper Point, but was there capsized by a tremendous sea. The seven men in the cockpit were

The Arab, *under sail, involved in a public relations excercise at Padstow. She was wrecked in April 1900*

flung clear but the four men battened below in the engine room were trapped. Four local women were widowed and fourteen children left fatherless by this appalling lifeboat disaster.

At St Ives, the little *Moses* lifeboat performed a magnificent rescue in Ocober 1865, when the French brig *Providence* was wrecked on the western spit of Hayle Bar. The lifeboat broke her drogue-rope in a heavy sea when crossing the Bar and, flying before the storm in an almost perpendicular position, overturned, throwing out all hands except the Coxswain and Second Coxswain, who remained under the boat for two whole minutes until she righted. The remainder of the crew regained the boat and after great difficulty managed to save one of the brig's crew, who floated to them on a raft, but two others were swept away and drowned. The *Moses* then again capsized, but righted in a minute; and the French captain and two seamen put off from the wreck in their small boat, which was swamped in the raging seas The lifeboat pulled to their assistance and picked them up, bringing all the rescued men safely to harbour. For this courageous piece of work the RNLI voted a silver medal to Coxswain Levett. Napoleon III, Emperor of the French, also sent a gold medal for the Coxswain and a silver medal for each of the crew, the first awards of their kind ever gained by British lifeboatmen.

St Ives

Constance Melanie *of Coverack. Coxswain John Corin, at the helm, received the RNLI silver medal after the rescue from the* Pindos *in 1907*

From 1901 to 1939

The opening of the twentieth century saw virtually the entire Cornish seaboard protected by a fleet of some nineteen pulling and sailing lifeboats. By 1939 this number was to be reduced by almost half, principally as a result of the introduction of motor lifeboats in the 1920s and 1930s – craft whose greater range and speed made it possible to give even better coverage from fewer stations. The necessary closures were nevertheless received with much local regret, representing as they did the ending of a long tradition of selfless and courageous public service.

Coverack   One new station was opened at the very beginning of this period – Coverack, in 1901. This old-world fishing village lies on the eastern side of the Lizard and the decision to place a lifeboat there was taken after the disastrous wreck of the *Mohegan* in 1898 and the stranding of the *Paris* in 1899. These revealed the need to supplement the coverage given to the Manacles by Porthoustock station. The first Coverack lifeboat, named *Constance Melanie,* performed her initial service on 13 January 1902 – saving sixteen lives from the barque *Glenbervie,* stranded at Lowland Point.

March 1907 marked one of the highlights of the *Constance Melanie's* career, for on the 17th she saved 44 lives from the wreck of the ss *Suevic.* Further laurels were added to her record on 10

February 1912, at the wreck of the 2,354 ton four-masted German barque *Pindos,* on Mear Point to the SW of Coverack. The lifeboat was launched at 9.45 pm in response to distress rockets, and found the vessel with huge seas breaking over her. After a tremendous struggle they succeeded in establishing communication with her, some German sailors pluckily throwing themselves into the sea to carry lines to the lifeboat. Four men were successfully taken off, but in the increasing SE gale the lines broke, and the lifeboatmen were so hampered by darkness that they decided to cease operations till daylight. However, aided by a powerful new type of acetylene lamp on shore, the coxswain and his men formed an endless whip by lines with a lifebuoy bent on, and by this means transferred the remaining 24 sailors to the lifeboat. For this fine rescue, carried out under extremely difficult conditions, Coxswain John Corin was awarded the Institution's silver medal.

On 26 July 1935, the inaugural ceremony of a new motor lifeboat called *The Three Sisters* was performed at Coverack. A particular Cornish interest attaches to this boat, for she was built out of a legacy from the late Miss Margaret Quiller-Couch, of Looe, whilst the name commemorated Maria, Sarah and Margaret, daughters of Richard Quiller-Couch, of Penzance. Sir Arthur Quiller-Couch formally presented and named the boat during a ceremony in the harbour.

An interesting event occured at the Cadgwith station during **Cadgwith** 1907, when the White Star liner *Suevic,* 12,500 tons, homeward bound from Melbourne, ran on the Clidgas Rock in thick fog during the night of 17 March. Both the Lizard and Cadgwith lifeboats launched through heavy seas whipped up by a strong SW wind. They found that two ship's boats had already been launched, filled with women and children. The Lizard boat towed one to Polpeor; and when it was realised that the liner had 524 persons on board, the Coverack and Porthleven lifeboats, plus tugs from Falmouth, were summoned. The work of rescue went on through the night, but high tide and incoming swells soon made landing impossible at Polpeor, so subsequently loads were taken to Cadgwith, the boats being assisted by tugs. All were safely brought ashore, the Lizard boat rescuing 167, Cadgwith 227, Coverack 44, and Porthleven 18. The remaining 68 were landed by the ship's boats and tugs. The Institution awarded a number of silver medals to lifeboatmen and others who had displayed great bravery in this memorable rescue operation. The after part of the *Suevic,* including the engines and boilers, was subsequently salvaged, the boilers being stoked up and the engines worked astern the whole way to Southampton, thus greatly assisting the tugs and relieving the foremost bulkhead of the strain of heading into the seas. With a new forward section specially built, the *Suevic* was back on her ocean travels before the end of the year.

The Lizard lifeboat Admiral Sir George Back *and crew, 15 February 1912, after her service to the barque* Chili

Lizard   At the Lizard station, several services to square-rigged sailing ships were performed between 1911-13. First, on the afternoon of 3 November 1911, the ship *Hansy*, of Fredrikstad, bound from Sweden for Sydney with timber, was stranded in a gale at Penolver and quickly began to break up. Most of those on board were rescued by rocket apparatus, but the Lizard lifeboat took off three. About three months later the French barque *Chili*, from Iquiqui for Falmouth for orders, became embayed in thick fog in Pentreath Bay in February 1912. The lifeboat was launched to her assistance, whilst four Falmouth tugs arrived later. With considerable difficulty, a hawser was passed to the *Chili* by the lifeboat, and the barque was eventually towed safely to Falmouth. On 5 May 1913, the fine four-masted steel barque *Queen Margaret*, homeward bound with wheat from Sydney, struck the Stag Rock, about a quarter of a mile out under the lighthouse. With water rising rapidly, the captain ordered the crew to take to the boats. The Lizard lifeboat was on the scene in half an hour, being first asked to land the master's wife and child. The ship settled down with a heavy list to port, and it became obvious she could not be saved. Returning, the lifeboat put lifeboatmen on two of the ship's boats to take charge while landing twenty men; then while the yards were actually touching the sea, the captain and four officers were taken aboard. The fourth square-rig disaster in this period of two years was that of the ship *Cromdale*, on 23 May, soon after the *Queen Margaret*. The greater part of the crew in this case were saved by the Cadgwith lifeboat.

During 1913 Frederick Pilley, of London, gave a sum of money for a motor lifeboat for the Lizard. At the time there were less than twenty of these craft around our coasts, and the decision was a token of the importance of this key station. New launching arrangements were necessary to accommodate this larger and heavier boat. A new house and slipway, 300 ft long, were constructed; and as it was impossible to rehouse in the normal way by hauling her stern first up the launching slip, it was decided to bring the boat ashore bows-first on the old concrete slipway. There she would be hauled up and through a starboard turn onto a turntable which, by turning and tipping, would allow her to re-enter the house from the back. The old lifeboat house was converted to take the powerful motor winch necessary for hauling. Owing to war conditions, however, the *Frederick H Pilley* motor lifeboat was not stationed at the Lizard till 1920.

This lifeboat and her successors performed many valuable services. In March 1921, 15 were saved from the *Gloaming*; in June 1923, 20 from the coaster *Nivelle*, of London; in August 1924, 93 from the ss *Bardic*, of Liverpool; and in June 1935, 38 from the tanker *D L Harper*.

Mullion

Of the other stations in this area, Mullion was closed in 1909, altered conditions in the immediate locality rendering its retention no longer necessary. Porthoustock lingered on until 1942, but performed only one life-saving mission during this century – on 4 August 1922, when eight were rescued from the ss *Dolphin*, the vessel herself also being brought to safety.

Looe

In south-east Cornwall, Looe station remained operational until 1930. Among the more interesting services performed were the saving of 19 from the ship *Gipsy*, in December 1901, and 21 from the French trawler *Marguerite*, in March 1922.

Polkerris

At Polkerris, the dwindling number of horses available during the First World War made it necessary to provide the station with pushing poles for launching. But this system was not satisfactory and accordingly a motor lifeboat was proposed. However, as light carriage-borne motor lifeboats were not then in service, this would have involved mooring the lifeboat in open water outside Polkerris pier, so it was eventually decided that Fowey harbour would be the best place for such a craft. The War having greatly delayed the motor lifeboat programme, the station at Fowey was opened in 1922 with a further pulling and sailing lifeboat, the *James, William and Caroline Courtney*. The first motor lifeboat arrived at Fowey in August 1928. Named *CDEC*, she was one of the 45 ft Watson cabin type with twin engines, giving a speed of eight knots and a radius of action of 100 miles.

Fowey

Mevagissey   The Mevagissey station closed in 1930. Among the more notable services performed were the saving of 22 from the steamer *Eastfield,* on 27 November 1917; of 13 from the steam trawler *Emerald,* of Boulogne, on 9 September 1923; and of 21 from the ss *Butetown,* of London, on 29 January 1918 – the last being performed by the motor fishing boat *Margaret* working under the RNLI Emergency Rescue Scheme.

Falmouth   In February 1914, the Falmouth station performed one of the most dramatic rescues ever accomplished by a Cornish lifeboat. The German four-masted barque *Hera,* bound from Pisagura in Chile, with nitrate, to Falmouth for orders, struck heavily on the Whelps, a submerged reef by Gull Rock, in Gerrans Bay, and sank in about ten minutes. Two boats were launched, and most of the 24 on board got into the one on the port side. Heavy seas quickly capsized this, however, and all were thrown into the bitterly cold water. Several managed to return to the barque, where the captain and a few others remained, whilst some succeeded in righting the boat and three or four got back into her, but she soon sank, all in her being drowned. The nine survivors then climbed on to the *Hera's* sloping jigger mast, and managed to attract the attention of people on shore by shouting and blowing a whistle. No help could be given to them from land, however, and with the sea gradually rising around them the first mate succumbed from exhaustion; the second mate and two seamen soon followed him. Meanwhile, the Portloe coastguard summoned Falmouth lifeboat, which reached Gull Rock at 3.30 am towed by the tug *Perran* through heavy seas. After a lengthy search in total darkness the wreck was located, and they managed to rescue those who still clung to it. Three men had dropped exhausted into the sea only minutes before the lifeboat's arrival.

The first motor lifeboat arrived in Falmouth in 1931. Named *The Brothers,* she had originally been built for the Penlee station in 1922, and was a 45 ft Watson type boat, carrying a crew of eight. Her only service was on 4 March 1932, when she launched to the ss *Ocklinge,* of London, ashore on Lowland Point. On arriving at the scene, however, she found the Coverack lifeboat in attendance and returned to station.

Porthleven   In the Mount's Bay area, the Porthleven station was closed in 1929, the motor lifeboats then in service at Penlee and the Lizard being considered to give sufficient protection to this stretch of

Penzance   coast. At Penzance, the *Elizabeth and Blanche* lifeboat was transferred to Newlyn harbour in 1908 to facilitate launching, this being the first move towards establishing the present Penlee station. Penzance was not immediately closed, however, a smaller self-righting rowing boat, the *Cape of Good Hope,* being placed there in case of accident or necessity. This boat having been damaged in service was replaced by the sailing lifeboat *Janet Hoyle* in 1912. On Boxing Day of that year she was launched during a 90 mph gale to the assistance of the Italian steamer *Tripolitania,* ashore on Loe Bar. The *Janet Hoyle* was signalled by rocket from Porthleven to return before she reached the wreck. She experienced terrible conditions on this service: the stemhead was split from the planking and two members of the crew died later from pneumonia.

The Penzance station was finally closed in 1917. Meanwhile the decision to form a station at Penlee had been taken as early as 1910. A house with direct slipway at this headland half-way between Newlyn and Mousehole was regarded as the best answer to local launching problems. The necessary shore establishment was built in 1912-13, the *Elizabeth and Blanche* being transferred from Newlyn in 1913. This lifeboat was replaced by the station's first motor lifeboat *The Brothers* late in 1922. She was of the Watson type, and the first to be fitted with the new 90 bhp 6-cylinder engine. She received a call to the dreaded Runnelstone on 8 October 1923, when the ss *City of Westminster,* bound from Belfast to Rotterdam with 73 on board, struck there in thick weather. Sennen Cove lifeboat arrived at 11 am and took off three women and ten of the crew, whilst the Penlee boat took on board a number of the crew who had left in their own boats, and then went alongside to take off the officers. The Penlee men saved 35, the remaining 25 being towed to port in their own boats by the Penzance steam drifter *Pioneer.* **Penlee**

Round the Land's End, at Sennen, extensive alterations were put in hand in 1919 to make the station suitable for a motor lifeboat, including the laying of a trolley way down the slip. The first motor lifeboat, named *The Newbons,* a 40 ft self righter, arrived in the spring of 1922. Between 1927-9 the station was entirely reconstructed to improve the launching arrangements. A long launching slip was provided plus a shorter hauling-up slip with turntable at its head for transferring the boat from one to the other. This represented a great improvement; but even today the boat cannot be launched for an hour and a half either side of spring low water and rehousing is also sometimes impossible during certain states of tide or weather. **Sennen**

At Scilly, both the St Agnes and St Mary's lifeboats were engaged on 20 September 1903 in one of the classic cases of salvage by the Islanders. The steel barque *Queen Mab,* of Glasgow, bound from South America for Falmouth, touched the Spanish Ledges, and began to leak badly. Aided by the steam packet *Lyonesse* the barque was towed into harbour, but was not brought safely alongside the quay until another tide had passed. Some useful sums were awarded to the owners of the *Lyonesse* and to the crews of the gigs and lifeboats for their assistance in various ways. **St Agnes** **St Mary's**

In December 1907, the huge seven-masted steel schooner

25

Henry Dundas, *the fourth of that name, launching at St Mary's, Scilly*

Thomas W Lawson – the first and last of her kind, and one of the wonders of the contemporary shipping world – bound with petroleum in barrels from Philadelphia for London, anchored in a rising gale on finding herself heading inside the Bishop Rock. Both Scilly lifeboats went off and reached her soon after dark. The master would not abandon ship, but accepted the offer of a pilot. The St Mary's boat struck the schooner's stern when coming in close to hail, carrying away her own mast, whilst one of the St Agnes crew collapsed, possibly with a heart attack, and both returned to base. During the night the gale gusted to 90 mph and the schooner was driven on to Minmanueth. On striking, most of the crew took to the masts, but she split in two and rapidly broke up. At dawn, the lifeboats, on putting out again, found nothing but vast quantities of wreckage floating in a sea of oil. The gig *Slippen* found a man alive on Annet but he died soon afterwards. The captain and engineer were washed on to Hellweather, but becoming unconscious were unable to make their presence known until a further day had passed. They were then saved at great risk by the *Slippen's* crew, and by F C Hicks gallantly swimming a deep gully between two reefs to take a rope to the Captain. He was a brother to the pilot who had earlier been put on board and was numbered among the fifteen lost. Hicks was awarded the RNLI's silver medal and a gold watch by the US Government, whilst the whole gig's crew received US gold medals.

In October 1919, the first motor lifeboat, named *Elsie,* arrived at
St Mary's. This innovation, together with the difficulty of getting
sufficient men for a crew at St Agnes, led to the latter station being
closed the next year. The *Elsie's* first important service was on 2
December 1920 when she saved 24 from the German steamer
Hathor. An even more notable rescue took place on 27 October
1927, on the occasion of the wreck of the steamer *Isabo,* of Lussin-
Piccolo, for which the RNLI awarded no less than two silver medals,
six bronze, and several vellums, whilst the Italian government sent
38 silver and bronze medals. The *Isabo,* laden with wheat, ran
ashore at 5 pm on the north side of Scilly Rock west of Bryher. The
gig *Czar* and motor boats *Sunbeam* and *Ivy* put off from Bryher,
the *Czar* rescuing eleven men floating on pieces of wreckage and
transferring them to the *Ivy.* Picking up three more from the sea she
passed a line on board the wreck and dragged another man to
safety. The *Ivy* found a man, and saved him, the *Sunbeam* also
saving one man from the water. The *Sunbeam* then launched a 9ft
dinghy which approached the wreck through the floating debris,
and in each of three sorties, executed under highly dangerous
conditions, took in one man, each having to be hauled carefully
over the stern to avoid capsizing the boat. While this was going on,
Sunbeam picked up another man and then, hearing cries from the
wreck, found a way to her stern, and drew seven men, including the
Captain, to safety by a line. The lifeboat arrived on the scene about
9 pm and found men clinging to the foremast, but conditions made
it impossible to approach. The lifeboat sheltered in New Grimsby
till dawn, then went to the wreck again and fired lines over her. One
of the survivors fell into the water while attempting to secure a line,
but was rescued unconscious. Two other men fell into the water,
and were similarly rescued. A fourth on the mast was dead. Shouts
were then heard from a rock, and they fired a line to a lone figure,
naked save for his lifejacket. He fell into the sea when attempting to
reach the line, but swam powerfully towards the lifeboat, and was
dragged in. It was later ascertained that six men were missing,
three of whom were probably drowned in the stokehold when she
struck.

In 1900 a new lifeboat was brought to St Ives which remained in
service there until 1933. Named *James Stevens No 10,* she achieved
a magnificent service record, saving several hundred lives and
assisting many vessels. One of her most dramatic services was to the
ss *Eleanor,* which, during the early morning of 22 December 1922,
sent up distress signals about eight miles NW of St Ives Head. She
had lost her propeller a few hours previously in a gale off Pendeen,
and was in a helpless condition. In appalling weather conditions,
the lifeboat made for the vessel under double-reefed canvas. The
Captain at first refused to come off, but as the lifeboat was leaving,
the ship's crew beckoned her to return, as they wished to be taken

James Stephens No 10, on the quay at St Ives. Notice the 'sand-plates' on the wheels, which helped transport the boat across soft sand or mud

ashore. The lifeboat accordingly went back and was hauled up the steamer with two grappling lines, and the men were told to drop into her whenever a chance presented itself. The *Eleanor* was rising and falling in the trough of the sea, which at times washed right over her. However, they had a little shelter under her lee, and some of the men dropped into the boat itself, others being caught by the lifeboat crew. When it was thought everyone else had left, the Captain himself came off, this operation taking about half an hour; but no sooner had they pushed off than three more men came out of the forecastle. Eventually, all sixteen hands were taken aboard, and the lifeboat returned to station. Meanwhile, the *Eleanor* continued to drift, and about two in the afternoon struck the Stones, near Godrevy Lighthouse. Terrific seas were breaking clean over Godrevy, and within half-an-hour these had pounded the steamer into a complete wreck.

The *James Stevens No 10* was replaced in 1933 by the first St Ives motor lifeboat, the *Caroline Parsons*. The career of this boat came to a tragic close on the last day of January 1938, when she was totally wrecked during the first of the two St Ives lifeboat disasters, which occurred within a year of each other. Just after seven in the evening during a severe storm the 3,700 ton Panamanian steamer *Alba,* bound from Barry to Italy, with coal, ran on rocks on the NW side of the Island. The lifeboat was promptly launched and battled her way through heavy seas until the steamer was sighted. Before getting under her lee, Coxswain Cocking ordered the anchor to be dropped and the line paid out, intending to use this when withdrawing from the wreck, but unfortunately the anchor failed to hold. The steamer's crew of 23 were taken on board, and the lifeboat then came astern on her engine, the anchor being useless. As she cleared the steamer's bow a tremendous sea struck broadside on, causing her to turn turtle and throwing nearly everyone on board into the sea. A line was thrown to her crew by the St Ives LSA team, and by its aid they were brought ashore, helped over the rocks by hundreds of local people, who braved the rough seas to assist them. Despite the heroic action of the townsfolk, many of whom risked their lives time and again to snatch the drowning seamen from the water, two were lost and three brought ashore dead, but all the lifeboatmen were rescued. The lifeboat herself became a wreck. Coxswain Cocking was awarded the Institution's silver medal and the crew bronze medals for this heroic service. The Hungarian government also presented a Gold Cross of Merit to Coxswain Cocking and a similar award to the Mayor of St Ives in recognition of the gallantry and courage displayed by the townsfolk.

The second disaster occurred on 23 January 1939. Just before two o'clock that morning a vessel was reported in a dangerous position NNE of Cape Cornwall. A gale of exceptional violence was then raging. When it became known at St Ives that Sennen lifeboat could not be launched owing to the low tide, Coxswain Cocking fired the assembly signal. Twenty minutes later the *John and Sarah Eliza Stych,* which had been sent to St Ives from Padstow as a replacement for the *Caroline Parsons,* was launched, with the assistance of eighty helpers. Off Clodgy Point a wave struck her on the starboard bow and she capsized. Being a self-righter, she came up again in a few seconds, but four of the eight men on board had been lost including the Coxswain.

The engine had cut off when the boat capsized, and could not be re-started as some gear fouled the propeller. They then dropped anchor and attempted to step the mizzen mast, but with half the boat's complement gone it proved beyond their powers. Flares were burnt, and seen from shore. The local LSA was immediately ordered out to Godrevy Point, and Penlee lifeboat launched at five o'clock. The lifeboat continued to drift across the Bay. A second sea struck her beam on, and she capsized a second time. When she righted, the motor mechanic had disappeared. As the boat approached the rocks near Godrevy the boat capsized for a third time; when she righted only one man, William Freeman, remained on board, the bowman and the assistant mechanic having been washed out of her. Three minutes later the lifeboat struck the rocks near Godrevy. As the sea receded, the one survivor crawled out and made his way on all fours along the rocks. A sea overtook him, but failed to knock him over. He scrambled up a gap in the cliffs, and made his way to Godrevy Farm where he told the tragic story of that night of death and disaster at sea.

St Ives After this second disaster the St Ives station was closed, although it re-opened as a 'temporary' war measure in 1940 since when it has remained operational.

Hayle In 1920 the Hayle station was officially closed, this step resulting chiefly from the decline in the coastal trade of the port. At

Newquay Newquay, two lifeboat accidents occurred, the first of these being on 6 March 1908, when the boat capsized during a practice launch and one member of her crew was drowned. The second took place in December 1917, when a large steamer, the *Osten,* appeared in distress off Penhale Point in a furious NE gale. The newly appointed Newquay coxswain said it would be impossible to launch as the gale was dead on the slipway, but former Coxswain J Gill got the boat away with a volunteer crew. She got well clear of the slip, but then a big wave slewed her round a little, and another sea caused her to heel over so that the sails were in the water, preventing her from righting. Eventually she righted herself and came in under the cliffs. All those in her were fortunately rescued from the shore, some noble and gallant work being done by the rescuers. The lifeboat – named *James Stevens No 5* – was, however, damaged beyond repair. Newquay station was closed in 1934, primarily as a result of local horses no longer being available for re-housing the boat.

Padstow At Padstow, following the tragic events of 1900, the RNLI decided to place a towed lifeboat at the No 2 station. The steam tug for towing this was named *Helen Peele* and the boat itself *Edmund Harvey.* For a period of twenty-eight years they sailed together in glorious partnership, achieving a remarkable record of distinguished rescues.   In 1929 No 2 station was supplied with a motor lifeboat. Named *Princess Mary,* she was the largest in the RNLI fleet at the time, being of the Barnett twin-screw type, 61 ft long, with two engines which gave a speed of $9\frac{1}{2}$ knots.   At Port

Port Isaac Isaac, considerable alterations were made in the arrangements for launching the lifeboat in the 1920s. A new boathouse was built at the bottom of the village and at the same time a breakwater was built out from the cliff on each side of the harbour. This did away with the picturesque scene which formerly was enacted each time the boat had to be dragged down to the beach through the narrow village street from the old boathouse higher up the hill. The station here finally became inoperative in 1933, when it was considered that the two motor lifeboats at Padstow could give protection to the area.

The number of services at Bude fell off considerably after 1900 and this station was closed in 1923.

James Stephens No 5 *at Newquay in 1901. She was damaged beyond repair in December 1917*

The Royal National Lifeboat Institution's lifeboats have, since its foundation in 1824, saved nearly 118,000 people.

In 1989 the cost of the lifeboat service, which relies entirely on voluntary contributions and legacies, exceeded £36,000,000. But 1988 was a prosperous year in lives saved: lifeboats went out 4273 times and no less than 1371 people were rescued. Inshore rescue boats – fast inflatable craft introduced in 1963 – went out 2379 times and saved 715 lives. The number of launchings has quadrupled in the last twenty years, and the demands on the service are greater than ever.

While you are in Cornwall, you will find many shops featuring collection boxes for the Institution. We hope you will take the opportunity to give generously.

The Lifeboat Enthusiasts Society was formed in 1964 to cater for those with a technical or historical interest in the lifeboat service. A long and interesting newsletter is published three times a year, covering a wide range of subjects including history, hull surveys, new lifeboats and equipment, building programmes and readers' letters.

The Society has its own archives section in which members are endeavouring to compile as near complete records as possible of lifeboat history. Technical information is also available which is of particular help to model-makers. For further details please write to the Honorary Secretary, John G. Francis, 13 West Way, Petts Wood, Orpington, Kent.

Lifeboat stations of Cornwall and the Isles of Scilly

Station	opened	closed	lives saved
Bude	1837	1923	56
Bude inshore lifeboat	1966		45
Port Isaac	1869	1933	86
Port Isaac inshore lifeboat	1967		100
Padstow No. 1 station	pre-1825	1967	163
Padstow No. 2 station	1899	1962	308
Padstow present station	1967		99
Newquay	1861	1934	92
Newquay inshore lifeboat	1965		202
St. Agnes inshore lifeboat	1968		118
Hayle	1866	1920	95
St. Ives	1840		628
St. Ives inshore lifeboat	1964		322
Sennen Cove	1853		302
Penlee	1913		322
Newlyn	1908	1913	72
Penzance	1803	1917	193
Porthleven	1863	1929	50
Mullion	1867	1908	3
Lizard	1869	1961	562
Lizard present station	1961		98
Cadgwith	1867	1963	388
Coverack	1901	1980	197
Porthoustock	1869	1942	127
Falmouth	1867		282
Portloe	1870	1887	0
Mevagissey	1869	1930	76
Polkerris	1859	1922	52
Fowey	1922		124
Looe	1866	1930	74
St. Mary's, IoS	1837		517
St. Agnes, IoS	1890	1920	262

Other books in this series include information about and photographs of many of the shipwrecks mentioned in this book, particularly:

Shipwrecks around the Lizard
Shipwrecks around Land's End
and *Tales of the Cornish Wreckers* tells the more gruesome story of earlier centuries.